Love is More Than a Word

Love is More Than a Word

Written by

Zachary Scott Rhiger

Illustrated by William Chappell

DEDICATION

I dedicate this book to all the people who have ever shown me love,
especially during the times when I couldn't bear to love myself.
Without your love, I would have never had the courage or the
inspiration to convert my buried emotions and lost thoughts
into poems, let alone write an entire book for others to read.
I am thankful for each and every one of you, and I hope
you are able to experience each aspect of love for yourself.

TABLE OF CONTENTS

PREFACE

Writing this book gave me the opportunity to share my feelings on the topic of love. This book contains personal thoughts and aphorisms, some of which you may have already thought about, a few that you have never considered, and others that you have yet to experience. The book also includes poems that illustrate a more vivid picture of love itself. After you finish reading this book, I hope you come to the same conclusion that I did - **love is more than a word**.

"So Simple"

Not one, not two, but three
Are all the words you need,
To say the most meaningful phrase
That will set anyone's heart ablaze.
Lets you say how much you care.
You can say it anytime and anywhere.
So simple, you might think it's too good to be true.
But honestly, all you have to say is "I love you."

The entirety of love cannot be explained by a single definition or a sole comprehension.

The only time you should lie is to protect a heart - not for evil gain or for your own benefit.

Always give your undivided attention to someone, or do not give any of your attention at all.

Only argue about the important things.

Being with someone you care about should never feel like an inconvenience.

Letting someone love you would be a lot less scary if you knew for certain that person was never going to hurt you.

"Unseen Inscription"

Don't give love up, and don't throw it away,
Because of what happened in the past.
Covert love is immutable, so make it last.
Take a smooth stone and inscribe your names,
To acknowledge a love that was never spoken,
Or heal a heart that feels shackled and broken.
A weight lifted with each letter etched in stone,
Realizing that you are free, but never truly alone.

All the things they love to watch, listen to, and partake in will eventually be all the things you enjoy too.

Offer up your jacket when you have the opportunity to.

If you really love someone, then you can't possibly love them any less.

Every day love a little more than yesterday.

Any time spent together should be cherished, regardless of how long it lasts.

Mutual respect is key in any relationship.

Never feel ashamed about being with the one you love.

What does love mean to you?

"Back to Reality"

Directly under the moonlight, fading in and out,
We sit on my car's hood atop the edge of the lookout.
The mood feels so right, like planets perfectly aligning.
I seize the moment, and lean in with a whisper
Of how I feel, hoping that I could maybe kiss her.
She turns her illuminated face, just smiling,
Without even muttering a word in return.
She softly pouts her lips undeterred.
Determined to press my lips against hers,
I lean in for a kiss to fulfill my heart's dream.
But her face slowly recedes into the moonlight,
Until the background is too bright to see. I screamed-
So loud, I woke myself up with such a fright.
I lie distorted at the very edge of my bed,
With a ray of sunlight peering directly on my head.
I'm so confused - was that a dream or a memory?

If you know that someone is attracted to you, either give them a chance, or set them straight.

Sincerely apologize. Otherwise, don't apologize at all.

The longer you wait to talk to someone, the harder it will be to say a word to them.

Find someone that takes your whole life to get to know.

What can I offer you that every other person hasn't already offered you before?

Be original. Don't copy what works for someone else.

A relationship should consist of you and me, and never anyone else.

What does love mean to you?

"A Moral Cuddle"

Is there such a thing as an innocent cuddle,
Or a way to sit close and nestle with each other?
Is it possible to bond with someone privately,
While avoiding the sins of our warped society?

Never feel like you need to prove yourself to someone. People should want to be with you for who you are.

Saying "Hey, I have feelings for you," is one of the scariest things you can say.

If I can see how perfect you are, why can't you?

Give second chances, because no one is perfect.

Love is the only emotion that you can simultaneously feel in your heart, mind, and body.

Never exploit another person's heart or feelings.

Do you ever stop and wonder why you actually love someone?

What does love mean to you?

"My Heart's Misfortune"

My heart has become rotten
From being neglected and forgotten.
It has repeatedly been thrown away
By those I love, and thus, continues to decay.
The pain makes it impossible for me to trust.
Eventually, my heart will turn into dust.
But maybe if someone along the way,
Sincerely loves me and decides to stay.
Perhaps the pain wouldn't be so unbearable,
And my heart could one day become repairable.

Random pickup line: Don't worry about other people judging you, because I would give you a 10 out of 10.

Your partner should be a constant reminder of all the things that you love too.

Hearts are fragile. Think about your actions before you shatter one into pieces.

Human nature can make us feel empty, alone, and lost without someone special in our lives.

Being in a relationship entails sharing everything, and not just the good stuff.

In a lasting relationship, you are obligated to stay the whole way, all day, and in every which way.

What does love mean to you?

"Time Well Spent"

I try to relive all the memories of me and you.
But as time passes by, my mind only recalls a few.
I hope that I never forget my favorite ones,
Because I want to relive them until they're gone.
Each and every one gives me a genuine smile,
A state of bliss that lasts quite a while.
So thank you for all the time we shared together.
I'll cherish these moments in my heart forever.

Don't hide away your true self for too long, or you will end up living a façade you cannot escape.

Love should never be taken for granted.

Relationships shouldn't be a game of they love me, they love me not.

Honesty is the best policy, but don't use it as a weapon.

Are you actually in love with them, or are you just in love with the "idea" of loving someone?

Love is a medicine that can be improperly administered.

Believe the truth, and not what you want to be true.

What does love mean to you?

"Bound to Me"

You are a bouquet of unforgettable memories.

You are a constant thought living inside of me.

I don't think about you only here and there.

I always feel you through me and through the air.

Not a moment passes by when I don't feel your presence,

Because you and me have become forever coalesced.

If you really want to be with someone, then you will make time for them no matter how busy you are.

Relational emptiness is the vacancy of someone that makes you feel whole inside.

Don't wish that you could have spent more time with someone or perhaps met them sooner, just enjoy the time the universe allotted for the both of you to be together.

Don't get tricked into believing that another person can break your heart, only love can break it.

Look for the reasons why a relationship will work, and not the reasons why it won't work.

You should always feel comfortable in the presence of each other.

"At Any Moment"

Every time you leave me to go on a trip,
I can't help myself - the tears start to drip.
I am certain you'll return to me in a few days,
Hopefully without any complications or delays.
But what if you were suddenly taken away?
Alas, a traveler's safety is never guaranteed.
I always treat these goodbyes like they're our last,
So I never have to question myself or even ask.
Did I say everything that was left in my heart,
Things, if unspoken, I would regret after you depart?

You can try as hard as you want to understand what love feels like, but you can't fully comprehend it until you experience love for yourself.

Compliments show that you notice the details.

Only say "I love you" to someone, if you truly mean it.

Never deny a loved one the chance to do something nice for you.

Learn to forgive completely; don't hold a grudge.

The very issues you keep locked away may come to light someday, and may inevitably push a loved one away.

What really causes love to manifest and grow inside a person?

"Difficult to Me"

To you, I might seem like a shy guy.

I can muster up a hello, and even a goodbye.

But having a conversation is quite difficult for me.

My words get jumbled up when you're all I see.

I know I shouldn't have to worry or fear,

But I don't want to say anything to upset you, my dear.

For you, it might be just a casual conversation,

But for me, it's a nervously, thought-out calculation.

Never keep your feelings hidden if you know you are going to regret never letting them out.

People come and go. Make sure you hold on tight to the people who you can't live without.

Love starts in the head, but matures in the heart.

Spend your time with someone you like, instead of wallowing over someone who doesn't like you.

You can't be distracted if you only have one person on your mind.

Always provide more than enough encouragement.

Love, without someone to love, is just a thought in your head.

"Wrong Timing"

I wish I could have said something in another life,
But I missed my opportunity to say "hi" twice.
I barely know you, and you barely know me.
I still can't stop thinking about you,
Because you are so damn pretty.
You are kind, funny, honest, and smart,
Which are all of my favorite qualities by far.
I could go on and on, but the bottom line is
Will I ever find someone as exquisite as you?

The time I spent being mad at you is the time I should have spent being happy with you.

Time is a limited commodity. Spend it wisely with the one you love.

First fall in love with what's on the inside, and then fall in love with what's on the outside. The inside usually remains the same, whereas the outside tends to change over time.

Visceral emotions should be tied to your favorite memories.

What others see as your faults, I see as your strengths.

Don't expect other people to change for you.

The only thing you need, in order to love a person, is an open heart.

"Unprocessed Information"

You were always hiding in the back of my mind,
But I never thought of you as the one I was trying to find.
You are everything that I have been longing for.
I can't believe I never realized it before.
Now I am convinced that you might be "the one."
I constantly think about you more than anyone.
But did I wait too long… have you found someone,
Or did I realize it just in time, before you moved on?

A good relationship should never have more painful memories than happy ones.

Actions speak much louder than words, so don't just say "I love you," show it.

True love shouldn't be one-sided; it needs to be shared.

Never sell your love, and never try to buy someone else's love.

What is your reason to keep on loving someone?

Love was intended for people, not objects.

Don't spend all your time worrying about someone else's life.

What does love mean to you?

"Wake-Up Call"

During the late hours of the night,
I was awoken by a horrifying fright.
I dreamt that you were taken away from me,
Believing it to be true, with half my bed left empty.
I was so petrified, I questioned if this moment was reality.
I hastily called your number, praying you were alive.
The phone kept ringing, 'til the silence ended with "hello."
The voice was hers, but the words were only a recording.
After the beep, I was too shocked to even say a word.
As the dark thoughts stirred, a faint voice was heard.
Her response was one of innocence and slight confusion,
But her answer did more than just lift my weighted burden.
This wake-up call revealed what I truly felt in my heart-
I can't go on any longer with the both of us living apart.

Find someone who will listen to you and help you with your problems, no matter how silly or serious they seem to be.

If you break her heart, her father will break every bone in your body.

Never let doubt change how you feel about someone.

Sometimes you have to step out of your comfort zone to feel comfortable with others.

What would you sacrifice for love?

I wonder if you think about me, as much as I think about you.

It doesn't matter how things starts; it only matters how they end up.

What does love mean to you?

"Stages of Loneliness"

Starts with a day when you're left all alone.

Turns into several days of being the only one home.

A few days turns into a month, and things only get worse.

Now another feeling comes into the picture - emptiness.

A month becomes a year, and you feel like there's nothing left.

All together these emotions have left you quite depressed.

But during this time, you still had the slightest tinge of hope,

Making you stay on life's metaphorical tightrope.

Finding reciprocal love is now your reason to keep on balancing,

The possibility of whether or not you can find love.

But as time passes by, it becomes harder to believe in chance.

So, I hope your odds change soon, before you fatally collapse.

One text, one compliment, just thirty seconds of your time is all it takes to make someone's day.

Showing love should never be reserved for only special occasions.

Surprise your partner with all the things you remember that they like.

Don't let the words that you never said hold you back from your potential.

Someone is truly special to you, if you can't see a future without them.

Being with you is so much fun that I never want it to end.

Love is only as strong as the bonds that comprise it.

"More Than a Friend's Love"

You are my friend and I am yours,
But some things in my heart I can't ignore.
I think you're funny and beautiful.
You make my heart thump like a bunny.
I wish I could tell you how I truly feel,
But then this secret would become real.
I will always continue to be your friend,
But I am so tired of playing pretend.
Telling you might jeopardize our friendship.
I couldn't live with myself if I ruined it.
I can't sit around and do nothing,
But I'm not sure what I should do.
It would be so much easier to commit,
If I knew you felt the same way too.

Public affection is a great way to show that you are not ashamed of or embarrassed by being with someone.

Don't listen to negative thoughts, especially when you're alone.

Love is not bound by time or distance.

It must be hard to notice if someone has feelings for you, because you can't see that I obviously do.

Don't be too blind to see what is right in front of you.

If you are going to love someone, love them unconditionally.

You are never just a little bit on my mind.

What does love mean to you?

"Reminders"

You inadvertently, cause me tons of frustration,
Because you refuse to see yourself as beautiful or special.
Perhaps I only think this way because of my predilection,
But one day, I hope, you will realize your true potential.
All the things I've said to you, I'll always believe are true.
It's the reason why I choose to constantly remind you.
I hope and pray for you every day that very soon,
You will come to love yourself as much as I do.

When you go out of your way to do something special for someone else, expect nothing in return from them.

Never let the sins and the distractions of this world come before the one person who is your whole world.

Relationships prosper when you both make an effort.

Learn to share your burdens, secrets, memories, experiences, and even laughter with each other.

Whenever you hurt someone, do your best to heal the wounds you have inflicted.

If you end a relationship, make sure you leave the other person in better condition than when you first met them.

What does love mean to you?

"My Love Is One of a Kind"

No one is ever going to love you,

Any more than I already do.

Others will say they feel the same way,

But do they love you every moment of every day?

Do they love you with all their might?

Does their love shine brighter than the moonlight?

I love you more than I love anyone else,

And I want you to know for yourself.

The best part of doing something special for someone is seeing the smile that you put on their face.

Constantly take pictures, because those memories are timeless.

It's not real love if you love someone else.

Things of the flesh only numb the pain temporarily, but love can make the hurt go away completely.

Never give up on the people who never stopped loving you.

Love keeps us grounded in reality.

What happens when your love is rejected by the one you love?

What does love mean to you?

"Two 'n Two"

I can't quite decipher this complex feeling,
But I know it arose when we first started meeting.
I feel it growing stronger the more I get older.
As time passes by, I become less emotionally sober.
This feeling takes a massive toll on my mind's gait,
Making it hard for me to even think straight.
I conclude that love might be this complex feeling,
But I won't know until time shows its real meaning.

A relationship should be treated like an investment. Only invest if you plan on keeping that bond for the rest of your life, and not for just a brief moment in time.

You should never be in a relationship that makes you feel ashamed.

Devotion for someone must be created with the purest intentions. Otherwise, it will become tarnished, and misconstrued into false worship.

Sometimes I need someone to hold me tight, and tell me everything is going to be alright.

If you never try, nothing will ever happen.

One of the hardest parts about loving someone else is the burden of knowing that one of you will beat the other to the grave.

What does love mean to you?

"Fluidity"

My dreams are the only place where I can be with you,
Ever since the day you were taken by the ocean's roar.
Now my heart feels like a victim of a constant tsunami,
Washing me up daily to shrivel on the trashed seashore.
The sight of you brings the raging waves tranquility,
But sadly, the water will not stay calm for very long.
When I awake, I'll go back to being the ocean's debris.
But it's comforting to know that I can still see you-
Even after you are done shimmering in the azure sea.

Don't change for the worse. I never want to leave you because you are not the person I fell in love with.

Going through a relationship alone defeats the very purpose of having a relationship.

A good place to have an uninterrupted conversation is in a parked car.

Love should never be a chore.

The purest memories are the ones that you never want to forget.

You'll never know if something will work out until you give it a try.

The more you love, the better you will love.

What does love mean to you?

"The Disguised Lie"

If you can look at someone for only a moment,
And be convinced that you are deeply in love.
Then you are only in love with the idea of them,
Because real love cannot be created on a whim.
It takes a little while to get to know someone,
Even longer to decide if they should be "the one."
But along the way, make sure that your emotions
Are real, and not deceived by false notions.
After some time has passed, you can decide for sure
If what you feel is a lie of the mind, or a love that is pure.

Always end a relationship on good terms because you never know what the future has planned for the two of you.

No one can help you, love you, or care about you until you can help, love, or care about yourself.

Pray every night for the person that you are meant to be with. Just because you don't know who they are, doesn't mean you can't start thinking about them today.

Once you start spending time with that someone special, being alone loses its appeal.

Scary situations become rewarding opportunities when you have the courage to seize the moment.

Be in control of your relationship, don't let others define it.

"In Color"

I am trapped in a lie that I can't escape.

I need someone to breathe truth into me before I suffocate.

The lie, I believe, is that I am destined to be alone.

Therefore, my life has become quite monochrome.

This lie controls my thoughts, influencing everything I do.

I can't change how I view life, without another's point of view.

That's why I desperately need someone to rescue me.

So I can finally be free, and see life more vibrantly.

Asking someone out implies that you've had the slightest thought of a future together. So if they reject you, it hurts not only because they said no, but because their rejection destroys a possible future for you.

Saying I love you, and proving that I love you, are two totally different things.

Treat others how you want to be treated. But don't love others how you want to be loved. Love them how they want to be loved.

The best moments are shared with people, but the best memories are felt with the heart.

If you make a mistake, you have no one to blame but yourself.

A relationship should never make you feel trapped or tied down.

What does love mean to you?

"Heart Condition"

Once your spirit breaks,
Your heart begins to deteriorate.
The pain becomes quite terrible,
And the damage seems irreversible.
But there's a way to neutralize the pain,
By finding a love that makes your heart beat again.
But don't wait too long, because soon may come a day
When your heart stops beating, and love will fade away.

Be aware of each other's weaknesses. You never want to unintentionally hurt someone where it hurts them the most.

Don't let the good times of yesteryear keep you stuck in the past.

Never be the reigning champion of the name game or the blame game.

Do you bring out the negativity or the positivity in people?

Look forward to the day when you find someone to experience redamancy with.

You never have to say goodbye, if you never leave.

Some emotions are better shared with others, not dealt with alone.

What does love mean to you?

"Stargazing"

I stare at the alluring stars in the night sky,

Just like I gaze upon your beautiful eyes.

Both jewels sparkle ever so brightly,

And gleam like the moon does nightly.

Every subtle intricacy is so enticing,

Uniqueness is what makes them mesmerizing.

To me, your eyes are a wondrous sight to see.

And that's why I can't stop myself from stargazing.

It takes one person, a few words, a couple seconds, and a lot of courage to make someone else no longer feel alone.

You don't have to be in a relationship to love someone with all of your heart.

People are only as important as you make them out to be.

If a person truly loves you, you can rest assured that you are being loved throughout the day, no matter where you are or what you are doing.

Facial expressions should complement the emotions you want to convey.

Learn to memorize all their favorite foods, songs, movies, etc. just for the sheer fact that remembering makes them happy.

"Not What You'd Expect"

I am the guy who will catch you off guard.

I will never purposely leave you scarred.

I am a gentleman, genuine and sincere.

I will stay by you side when others disappear.

I will always have your best interests in mind.

Never worry about me putting you in a bind.

I am nowhere near perfect, but I'm better than most.

If you give me a chance, I'll show you I never boast.

Love in such a way that it sets a proper example of how to love.

Learn each other's love languages, and adapt to each of them accordingly.

Learn to love in the moment, because tomorrow is never guaranteed.

Love regardless of how much someone loves you back.

The outcome you imagine is rarely the one you get.

If you are spending time with someone, they should never feel alone.

Don't be afraid to share the burden of someone else's pain.

"Missed Opportunities"

I was going to give you a hand-picked bouquet of roses,

But I waited too long for the right moment, so they wilted.

I was going to give you a hand-written card for your birthday,

But I thought too hard about what to write, so now it's belated.

I was going to sit down right next to you and start a conversation,

But I couldn't think of what to say, so now the seat is taken.

I spent too long wondering about what I should say and do,

Instead of actually spending that time with you and only you.

Hurtful words don't always need to be uttered aloud.

You never know until you try, but how do you go about trying something you don't know how to do?

Love keeps you warm on the nights when you are alone.

Sometimes life only gives you one chance.

People who genuinely try to be a part of your life are the people that you should give a second chance to.

Life is the beginning, and death is the end. Love creates life, and love continues beyond death.

Never assume that people know exactly how you feel.

What does love mean to you?

"Time's Uncertainty"

We have spent so much time together,
Doing things in hot and cold weather.
The whole time we were just friends,
But now I see you through a different lens.
I know I want to be with you romantically,
But I don't know if you feel the same about me.
I want to change just hanging out into going out,
But deciding how to tell you gives me doubt.
Do I ask you out on a date during the weekend,
Or skip ahead and ask you to be my girlfriend?
Both are plausible options, but whichever one I take,
I hope I make the right choice, not a horrible mistake.

Inevitably you will fight, but don't fight with uncontrolled anger and belittling. Fight with love and respect.

I am not trying to fill the hole in my heart with just anything. I am trying to fill it with what made the hole in the first place - you.

Don't make promises that you know you can't possibly keep.

Wanting to spend time with someone and wanting to spend every moment with someone is the difference between wanting a friendship and wanting a relationship.

Never be the reason why someone can't open up their heart to another person.

Mistakes should always be called out, and should never be left unattended.

What does love mean to you?

"Transfigured Perception"

Everyone used to think of you as quite plain.
Because of this notion, I sadly believed the same.
I adopted others' perceptions as my own,
Consciously making your true identity unknown.
Until one day, when I contemplated what I was feeling.
And surprisingly, hidden emotions started revealing.
Truth be known, my brain was forever rewired,
And you became the only person I truly desired.

If someone wants to be with you, you shouldn't have to beg them to spend time with you.

Pursue someone who appreciates you.

Being scared is normal sometimes; but you should never let fear keep you from making an important decision.

Don't focus on what you should have done in the past; focus on what you can do now.

Never intentionally make someone cry.

Don't share your heart if you're just going to be heartless.

When people truly depend on you, try not to let them down.

"The One That Got Away"

How often do you let someone slip

Through your very fingertips?

The person who could have been the one,

But now they have sadly moved on.

How often do you think about them,

Even though it was way back when?

The very relationship you let fall apart,

That still holds a special place in your heart.

When you are awake, you think about the things that you would like to have in life. But when you are asleep, you oftentimes dream about the things that your heart desires most.

At times, relationships can be emotionally draining, but they should also be equally fulfilling.

In a lasting relationship, love should always be reciprocated.

Never intentionally neglect someone.

Never give up on someone who never gives up on you.

Love prospers with an open heart, but flounders with a closed one.

Cheeks are meant to be red, but never black and blue.

What does love mean to you?

"French Brew"

Another day at my local coffee shop,
I order my favorite drink and sit at my usual spot.
Before I indulge in my very first sip of froth,
My eyes curiously decide to look up.
I notice an unfamiliar girl entering the store,
Hesitantly deciding where to sit on her own.
Surrounded by complete strangers,
Unlike her, I have already had the chance to know.
Her current scenario I experienced long ago,
Overwhelmingly compelled me to leave
My drink and greet her with a genuine hello.
To my surprise she responded with "bonjour,"
Which intrigued me more than anyone else had before.
I eagerly asked if I could sit and have a drink with her.
In English, she eloquently replied with "sure."
I started the conversation off with simple questions,
That I was so curious to know. From France she had come
And back she must go, for today was the last day
Anyone here had the opportunity to really know her.
We started talking when my drink was still steaming,
Until the moment the barista poured the night's last drop.
Upon leaving the shop, we parted with farewell goodbyes,
Starting a relationship that would last the rest of our lives.
We created a memory, in which I was enthralled so much,
That the contents of my coffee cup were left untouched.

Never be late. You never know when you might miss out on something amazing.

Don't search for love so intensely, because love usually ends up finding you instead.

You can never completely comprehend or relate to the pain someone else feels, but you can try your best to show them you care and will willingly bear their pain with them.

You can try to make plans for yourself, but remember life doesn't always make the same plans with you.

Why do you choose to care when it's so easy not to care?

Don't wait to love, miss, and care about someone while they are alive. It won't matter when they are gone.

What does love mean to you?

"Left Too Soon"

I will never hold you in my arms again,

Because our story has reached its end.

I wish you didn't have to leave so quickly,

Although our time together felt like an eternity.

But I know that you will always be here with me,

In the two places that matter, my mind and my heart.

If you need the love of more than one person, then you probably haven't experienced the right kind of love yet.

Love is free, but it will cost you your heart.

It's always better to fall in love together, than to fall in love by yourself.

Attraction and interest make you want to get to know someone for a day, but love makes you want to get to know them for the rest of your life.

Make sure to say "I don't love you" before someone falls hard for you, and says "I love you" first.

Love is choosing to stand by someone's side during a difficult situation, and not trying to fix their problems for them.

What does love mean to you?

"Roads Traveled"

Old roads are filled with dangerous potholes.
You try to walk over them, but they hurt your soles.
Paths that lead to a once-cherished destination,
Bring you only heartache and much devastation.
Try to find some fresh and well-paved roads,
Ones that are free of ditches and crossroads.
Don't waiver from the search for the safe path ahead,
Or you will never experience any ease on your tread.

During all the times when I had nothing to do and no one to talk to, I still had the thought of you to keep me company.

Time machines don't exist, so think before you make a final decision.

Is your love shown, or is it only spoken?

Letting someone into your mind is easy, but letting someone into your heart is difficult. Getting someone out of your head is attainable, but getting someone out of your heart is impossible.

Don't spend all of your precious energy worrying about me worrying about you.

Don't be the tissue that wipes away their tears; be the reason they need not cry in the first place.

"Why Don't You Care?"

Whenever I am feeling down and lonely,

All I want is for someone to notice me.

I can't seem to help myself when I feel this way.

How I need someone to help me on those dark days!

The people close to me are too blind to see I'm suffering,

But with all their smarts, they still choose to do nothing.

So, I guess I don't just want others to notice me,

I want people who actually care about me wholeheartedly.

I would rather experience a real and lasting love, than a fling to fill the void and heal the temporary sting of loneliness.

Don't be afraid to say the following things: I made a mistake, I need help, and I'm sorry.

A relationship is not a game, so don't keep score.

I don't think I will ever get over you, simply because I don't want to.

Always be true to your emotions, and upfront with your intentions.

Love persistently, consistently, and efficiently.

Your eyes are meant for one, not two, and definitely, not for a few.

What does love mean to you?

"We All Need Someone"

Your phone screen overflows
From a continuous downpour.
Tears, dropping one after the other,
Completely drenching your keyboard.
You struggle to compose a message,
But you can't for so many reasons.
Your screen is too wet to type on.
You can't see out of your puffy, bloodshot eyes.
A hundred painful thoughts run through your head,
Each prodding and stabbing away at your heart.
But most of all, you have no one to read your text
Detailing just how unstable you are right now.

True love creates an unbreakable bond between a couple; one that is not bound by the things of this world.

Love is a constant search for the cure we believe exists in the realm of fantasy, but actually only exists in the heart of one's own reality.

Never miss an opportunity to dance.

When I sleep, I dream about you; but when I wake up, I forget all the dreams I had about you.

Love should be free and boundless, lighting up the darkness. Love should be pure and faithful, always emanating something beautiful.

Don't make the mistake of playing pretend for too long, because you won't be able to identify real love when it's right in front of you.

What does love mean to you?

"Straight Ahead"

Always keep your eyes focused on the prize.
Don't be misguided by all the enticing lies.
Your heart will lead you towards the reward,
But only your spirit will guide you forward.
Don't be fooled by all the earthly distractions,
Or you'll get lost at one of life's many junctions.

Love at the very core of its existence is simple and pure, but the world tends to make it seem so difficult and tainted.

Never continue an argument that you know you can't win.

People find love distasteful when they have experienced a bitter breakup. But since love forgives everything, people can let go of anything. So don't blame love, blame your own refusal to forgive.

Who will your last thought be of - the person who you love the most or the person who you regret loving?

Keep a list recalling the dates of all of your firsts.

Love is a sacrifice that you willingly choose to make daily for the rest of your life.

What does love mean to you?

"Negligent Injury"

Your deepest wound has been left alone for so long,
That you can't tell something is definitely wrong.
I can see your heart is still bleeding quite profusely,
Because others have handled it quite abusively.
You are in desperate need of a new tourniquet,
But your heart is afraid of letting anyone touch it.
If you would give me a chance to stop the bleeding,
I promise to heal your heart so you can start re-living.

Decisions have consequences. But if you never take any action, nothing will ever happen.

Be your partner's number one fan, best friend, and one and only admirer.

Repetition can make relationships stronger, but it can also make relationships stagnant.

Is what you hold most precious in life, the person who you love the most?

Love is wrong if you don't have the right person to love.

Not everything can be fixed by experiencing love, but love can make any situation better.

What does love mean to you?

"Never on Purpose"

Hurtful mistakes are often made,
And the scars they leave slowly fade.
You can apologize, but be sincere
Or they might not believe you out of fear.
You can't take back the things you've done,
But you can stop yourself from making a "re-run."

69

Everybody is loved by at least one person, but how often do you stop to realize just how much they actually love you?

Don't compare relationships.

Don't be afraid to speak up now, because your hesitation could lead to a problem later.

Love was never intended to be short-lived.

You will never find the perfect moment to tell someone how you feel, so don't wait.

Know the difference between feeling love, and being in love.

Sorry® is a game, but when I say "I'm sorry" it's the real thing.

What does love mean to you?

"A Justified Reaction"

Every time I see you, you have this radiant glow,
Which causes my heart to beat out of control.
My hands sweat profusely, my head starts to swell,
Feels like everything else is going awry as well.
One by one, my emotions sway involuntarily,
My body is breaking down with such celerity.

You never have to say "I will never leave you again," if you don't leave in the first place.

Love knows when to put others first.

If you knew that someone you know wasn't happy, would you go on with your day? Or would you be sad knowing that they're unhappy, and go out of your way to make them feel better?

The purest conversations are not scripted.

Listen to remember, and not to forget.

No one will ever doubt you if you don't give them a reason to.

Your love for someone isn't meant for others to understand.

What does love mean to you?

"Out of Your Way"

You could have easily become a lost memory,
But you went out of your way to impact me.
You did your best to make yourself hard to forget,
And in the process, made me glad that we met.
Now you always seem to be on my mind,
Because you purposely made our lives intertwine.
I don't exactly know why you chose to do this,
But I can't thank you enough for giving me true bliss.

Don't miss out on making memories because you were too busy adoring your phone.

A relationship entails two people: you and someone who will always have your back.

It's natural to gaze upon another when you are in a relationship, but never act upon it.

Love stings, hurts, and burns; but love will not kill you.

Some of your secrets and stories will never be told to anyone, but don't be so afraid of sharing them that you never open up at all.

Be proud of your relationship; don't be afraid to share your loved one with the world.

What does love mean to you?

"Impasse"

I can't contemplate the idea that you are gone.

Undoubtedly, I don't know how to move on.

I used to spend every day loving you with all my heart.

Now I can only love you as a memory; it's tearing me apart.

How am I supposed to function throughout the day,

When my only reason to live has gone away?

A resolution surely exists. Shall I bear the pain?

I don't know with this condition, I can withstain.

If I am in love with someone who doesn't love me back, am I being ignorant or am I being patient?

If you think love is a lie and nothing feels real, then explain to me why my heart pounds so loudly only when I'm with you.

Saying I will treat you better implies that I didn't treat you right before.

Love isn't just a one-time thing. You have to continue to love every day, and even more, with each passing day. But the longer you love, the easier it becomes.

Sometimes, love requires you to wait patiently.

Love can be hard to express for some people, but when they do eventually show it, their love should be appreciated and cherished.

"Fading Features"

I try to picture you in my favorite memories,
But I can't seem to recall every detail.
I have forgotten the charm of your smile,
The gleaming intricacies in your eyes,
The mood you were in, happy or sad,
And your outfit, dressed up or dressed down.
I try my best to remember each moment,
But time seems to have erased quite a few.
The only constant feature I can't forget,
Is the love shared between me and you.

Days are priceless in a relationship that lasts a lifetime.

It's always a perfect time to do something special for someone special.

Love never gets tired of what it sees.

If you need a sign to know that you are loved, then you are probably not truly loved.

Don't make silly mistakes for the so-called sake of love.

Don't be afraid of letting your heart break, because the scars will make you stronger.

Find someone who makes saying "goodbye" almost unbearable.

What does love mean to you?

"Mask of Lies"

I turned into someone that you would be interested in,
Because I was ashamed of who I was under my skin.
I had no idea that we would be together this long.
And now, you truly believe that I am fearless and strong.
I am scared that it's too late to unveil my disguise,
Because if I were to take it off, it could be our demise.
You would have to say goodbye to the mask you know so well,
And be disappointed to see underneath, I am just a hollow shell.
I realize that I should have been honest from the beginning,
But would you have accepted me if I wasn't pretending?

If I could be anywhere in the world right now, I would be wherever you are.

Don't let your emotional scars be more prominent then the scars on your skin.

I want to be able to give you the world, but sometimes the only thing I can offer up is myself.

Love requires an open and willing heart.

People won't have a clue about your intentions if you never make them known to anyone.

What is your heart saying right now - is it revealing an emotion, a name, a place, or a memory?

"Never Stop Searching"

You can't wait around all day
And expect love to just come your way.
Love is something that you have to pursue,
Especially when you feel that it's long overdue.
So don't give up when the search starts to get tough,
Because you will regret not trying hard enough.
Remember, once you find the love you're looking for,
You won't have to aimlessly search the earth anymore.

Love is doing things regardless if anyone else ever knows that you did them.

Set your own goals and dreams, but don't forget to share a few of them with someone else.

Who is the one person that holds the key to your heart?

You will know when you find the right person when you don't want anyone else.

All I want for my last day on earth is to be surrounded by all the people I love, and who truly love me.

Love allows others to make decisions on their own. Not every decision should be approved or persuaded by you.

"The Unheard Conversations"

It is perfectly normal to have moments filled with silence.

Don't feel pressured to talk when the conversation seems quiet.

Stop to enjoy the moments, and listen to what the details have to say.

Can you hear her smile telling you she's having a wonderful time?

What about her eyes saying you look handsome today?

Details are always talking, but they are not always listened to.

I guess that silence is never truly silent in any conversation,

So make sure you are always listening attentively in every situation.

Learn from, don't harp on past loves. Focus on, don't compare your present love.

Follow your own heart, not the heart of another.

Don't be afraid to wait to get into a serious relationship, to get engaged, or to get married. The right person won't care how long it took, since they are planning on spending the rest of their life with you.

Love allows us to care about what is on the inside of a person much more than what is on the outside.

You should never tire of loving someone.

Look forward to making plans and setting dates for your future together.

What does love mean to you?

"Never Do Drugs"

I decided to leave you because I was addicted to your drug.

A narcotic that gave me a false sense of happiness and fulfillment.

It clouded my judgment, and altered every decision I made.

This substance consumed my thoughts, my money, and my time.

It controlled every aspect of my life without me realizing it.

I guess that's what happens when you're addicted to an impure love.

Count yourself lucky if you find love, because there are thousands of people still frantically searching for love at this very moment.

Don't wait for the one you love to say "I love you." Make sure to say it first.

Don't hold your love up to the standards and expectations of other people.

True love comes naturally.

The best part about spending time together is creating a memory with you.

Love seems scary to some people because they are afraid of things that they can't control.

"Street Art"

You are an artistic beauty,
Something only the eye can see.
Just like chalk art on the street,
You will never be quite complete.
When rain washes part of you away,
Your beauty doesn't seem to fade.
I'm glad that your artist created you,
Infatuated am I by your amazing hues.

Our days are numbered, so make sure you love when you have the chance to love.

Treasure is a lot like love; first it's lost, then it's found, and sometimes it's buried again.

Love that gets violent isn't love at all.

Know when you should beg for them to stay, and know when you should let them go.

You should be the best version of yourself whenever you are with the best part of your life.

When I miss a chance to spend time with you, I feel like I am being robbed of an opportunity to make another memory with you.

What does love mean to you?

"A Remainder of One"

In your life, you will meet a few
People who say they care about you.
Less will be honest from the start.
Fewer will actually win your heart.
Some will accept you with all of your flaws,
But only one will remain, and never withdraw.

You can never say the following words too much in your lifetime: "please," "thank you," and "I love you."

Love does not come with a pre-routed map; you have to figure it out along the way.

Love, as if no one else is looking, or listening.

As technology advances, couples will slowly cease to remember what it's like to have a real face-to-face conversation or to open a hand-written sentiment.

If you have to break up with someone, make sure you break up together, and not by yourself.

Life becomes easier to remember when you have someone memorable to spend it with.

What does love mean to you?

"Hopelessly Searching"

My heart is in an inescapable bind,
Because I yearn for the one I can't find.
I'm tired of searching day in and day out,
Only to come up short, no matter the route.
I am so exhausted of walking this life alone,
I just want someone who's real - flesh and bone.

Simple words, wholeheartedly spoken, oftentimes have a bigger impact than convoluted sayings.

Don't say you love someone if you are not ready to.

There are so many different ways to show you that I love you, but I only know one way to say "I love you."

If you kidnap my heart, make sure you take me too.

Together, two fractured hearts heal faster than by themselves.

Days go by way too fast when I'm with you.

Take a chance on love, but don't gamble your love away.

What does love mean to you?

"Important to Me"

It's the little things you do that make me smile-
Holding my hand as we walk down an aisle,
Telling me first all your good and bad news,
Complimenting insignificant things like my shoes.
Nevertheless, it's not the big things that give me delight,
But rather the small moments we share each day and night.

I think the feeling of loneliness never truly goes away, until you are able to spend a lifetime with someone.

Be comfortable being vulnerable, because it's harder to open up when you put up a brick wall.

Don't wait too long to realize how special someone is to you.

Only give compliments to others that you believe yourself.

When you find yourself in a rut, don't give up. Ask a close friend to help you out.

When I hold your hand, I really do have everything at my fingertips.

Love is way more than just a word.

What does love mean to you?

"Eye to Eye"

Oh friend of mine, I didn't see you yet.

But now I stare, a secret I wish I kept.

Opening my heart to another close by,

I said too much to a talkative, young guy.

He alluded my intentions to you quite blatantly.

Although, I had yet to realize what you meant to me.

Something exists for sure, but we still need to clarify

All of the unknowns. Is your gaze not set on another guy?

But the outcome I feared and expected to regret,

Is so much different than the response you did project...

My eyes have shifted to you as of late, still unsure

Of how to look, but that eye candy was a definite mistake.

I need some time to re-find my reflection in life's mirror,

Before I can see you altogether. Would you please consider?

My burdens will be lifted and paid for on the Ides of March

A clean conscious, a fresh start. Why, of course, I said yes.

Almost a year has passed since I heard your hopeful lie.

Here I am, still faithfully waiting for you, more or less.

But deep inside, I knew you were always cross-eyed.

Love is More Than a Word

What does love mean to you?

EXTRAS

What does love mean to you?

"Coping Mechanisms"

Life was designed to leave average people hollow-
People created without the slightest idea of how
To feel completely whole. I believe wallowing in isolation
Is the quickest fix to a breakup, rut, and even depression.
But my not-so average friends have their own secret solution,
They vouch will prevent me from feeling completely useless.
Elvis claims taking a far-out trip on a foreign plane
Transcends all the dark thoughts from one's brain.
Mary Jane asserts planting herbs in her secret garden
Creates the perfect aromas to take the edge off any burden.
Caine swears eating sweets with powdered sugar on top,
And an ice-cold Coke, make the pain come to a complete stop.
Walter vows his homemade crystal-based incense
Ends any problem so fast with the longest lasting effects.
Although my friends prescribed, advice from their gained wisdom.
They only gave me a quick fix to their "self-proclaimed symptoms."
Nothing is a cure, and yet, everything can be used to help us cope.
What is the one thing you embody, and then administer as dope?

Love is More Than a Word

What does love mean to you?

"Lollipop"

Two local boys venture into the county bar
Just past the usual bedtime for a school night.
Trying to locate two open, cherry leather seats,
Their eyes scan up and down the crowded counter.
Once they settle in, the scrawny boy on the left
Hastily reaches into his pocket for a box of cigarettes.
Inside were his special cigs with a wrapper over the top,
Rather than ones with the usual amber-colored filter.
He grabs a cig for himself, and another for his friend.
They remove the wrappers instead of using a lighter.
Both toss the allusive treats in the grooves of their incisors
Like dropping lit cigarettes in the teeth of an astray.
As the cigs become soggy, the boys' sweet tooths
Start craving the pleasures of a sinless virgin.
The bartender concocts a round of piña coladas
For them to indulge in. After their thirst is quenched
And their cigs lay bare, they pay the bartender
With all their chump change and monopoly money.
Then the boys throw their crumpled buds in the trash
And leave the bar with their addictions suppressed.

Love is More Than a Word

"Reflections"

As each year comes to an end,

We naturally reflect and ponder

About all the things that could have been.

If only we had a little bit longer

Or were prepared enough not to falter.

But don't fret, a new year is upon us

With ample opportunities for mistakes and successes.

The decisions we make are influenced by our past.

The examples set by a father will always last-

In the back of our minds to help shape our future.

Learn from his success story so that your life may go smoother,

And not from his mistakes that will only leave you with sutures.

Our fathers are role models, present or not, in our minds and hearts.

Let's reflect on the lives they lived before each new year starts.

Love is More Than a Word

What does love mean to you?

"Emotional Rollercoaster"

I wish I cried more.

I wish I shared my heart.

I wish I never moved so fast.

I wish I was loved by you more.

I wish I never told you how I felt.

I wish I never moved away from you.

I wish I was never misled by your texts.

I wish I was able to make you smile more.

I wish I never realized you had feelings too.

I wish I never had a reason to get that drunk.

I wish I had someone to lay with on the couch.

I wish I had a reason to wake up in the morning.

I wish I was able to find someone to call my own.

I wish I got another opportunity to say I love you.

I wish I had a reason to care about and love myself.

I wish I never heard you compare me to your first ex.

I wish I cashed in all the rainchecks you wrote out to me.

I wish I could explain everything that I keep hidden inside.

I wish I can one day look back at my life and not wonder why.

What does love mean to you?

"Behind the Scenes"

As you slowly slip off each garment down your sides,
And step into the hot shower with me waiting inside,
I finally see you bare, your body's secrets reside
Completely vulnerable, nothing left for you to hide.
The absence of hair and old wounds on your thighs
Show your conscious of other's judgmental eyes.
The healed, yet visible, scars on your voluptuous hips
Scream you survived a parent's beatings and whips.
The topcoat of polish painted on your nails each day
Masks all the stress bites and nibbles that chip away.
The flower tattoo hidden by the lace of your bra
Reveals added beauty, perhaps you're an outlaw.
The high-end makeup running down your face
Unveils imperfections, only you see as a disgrace.
Shower's done, your body is silky-smooth and clean.
Displaying your figure with trust, it can't be unseen.
The moment's passed, you pretend I don't matter;
Ignoring me, you leave the shower veiled in water.
You dry off, hugging the towel tight over your chest
Going back to how you were before, impeccably dressed.

Love is More Than a Word

Made in the USA
Monee, IL
05 December 2019

18025621R00072